# Inside the Mind of
# A CLEVER DOLPHIN

## TOM JACKSON

ANIMAL INSTINCTS

PowerKiDS press
New York

Published in 2012 by The Rosen Publishing Group, Inc.
29 East 21st Street, New York, NY 10010

Copyright © 2012 Wayland/The Rosen Publishing Group, Inc.

Editor: Julia Adams, Julia Quinlan
Book Design: Paul Cherrill

Photo Credits: All images and graphic elements: Shutterstock, apart from: p. 8 (inset): Paul Souders/Corbis; p. 11 (all insets): iStockp. 2 (top): iStock; p. 5 (all outlines): Wikimedia; p. 6 (inset): iStock; pp. 6/7: Jeffrey L. Rotman/Corbis; pp. 10/11: WILDLIFE GmbH/Alamy; p. 11: Eco Images/Getty; p. 12: iStock; p. 13: Stephen Frink/Corbis; p. 14 (inset): Dreamstime; pp. 14/15: iStock; p. 17 (inset): Martin Camm (WAC)/naturepl.com; pp. 18/19, p. 19 (inset): Flip Nicklin/Getty; pp. 20/21: Norbert Wu/Getty; p. 21 (inset, bottom): Terry Whittaker/FLPA; pp. 22/23: Peter Arnold, Inc./Alamy; p. 26, 27: iStock; pp. 28/29: Nic Bothma/epa/Corbis; p. 28 (inset): David Fleetham/Alamy; p. 29 (inset): Andy Rain/epa/Corbis.

Library of Congress Cataloging-in-Publication Data

Jackson, Tom, 1972–
  Inside the mind of a clever dolphin / by Tom Jackson. — 1st ed.
      p. cm. — (Animal instincts)
  Includes index.
  ISBN 978-1-4488-7034-9 (library binding) — ISBN 978-1-4488-7078-3 (pbk.) — ISBN 978-1-4488-7079-0 (6-pack)
  1.  Dolphins—Juvenile literature.  I. Title.
  QL737.C432J286 2012
  599.53'15—dc23

                              2011028819

Manufactured in the United States of America

CPSIA Compliance Information: Batch #WW2102PK: For Further Information contact Rosen Publishing, New York, New York at 1-800-237-9932

# CONTENTS

# Clever Dolphins

Dolphins are very clever animals, but they are smart in a different way than people. They communicate with sounds that we can barely hear. They also use noises to catch and kill **prey** – and they can even see inside a body!

Dolphins are **mammals**, which makes them related to animals such as dogs, squirrels, and humans. They belong to a group of sea mammals, called toothed whales.

**Dorsal fin**

**Smooth skin**

**Tail fluke**

Beak

Flipper

Unlike land mammals, dolphins have no hairs. Smooth skin is better for swimming in water. Dolphins have a layer of fat, or blubber, under their skin to keep out the cold.

## MEET THE TOOTHED WHALES

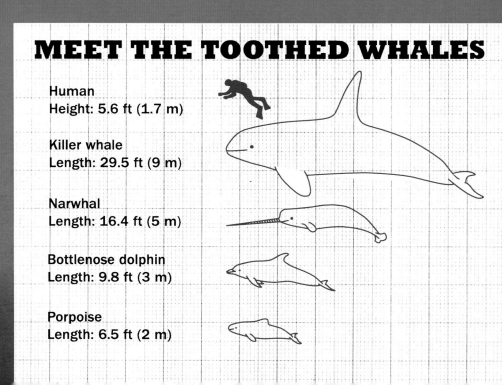

Human
Height: 5.6 ft (1.7 m)

Killer whale
Length: 29.5 ft (9 m)

Narwhal
Length: 16.4 ft (5 m)

Bottlenose dolphin
Length: 9.8 ft (3 m)

Porpoise
Length: 6.5 ft (2 m)

# Born to Swim

Bottlenose dolphins give birth underwater. As soon as the baby is born the mother pushes it to the surface so it can breathe.

Like other mammals, baby dolphins drink milk from their mothers.

The dolphin mom pushes its young to the surface of the water because it cannot swim well yet.

Calves stay close to their mothers so they do not get lost.

Dolphin milk is very fatty. It helps build up the young dolphin's layer of blubber. A baby is suckled by the mother for 18 months.

A young dolphin, or calf, stays with its mom for about five years.

7

# Taking the Air

Dolphins and other toothed whales evolved from a mammal that lived on land. Even though they live in water, dolphins still breathe air just like their land relatives.

Dolphins do not have to breathe through their mouths. They have special holes in their heads, called blowholes. All they have to do is bring their blowhole to the surface of the water and take a breath.

A dolphin breathes through a blowhole – a large nostril on top of the head.

The leap-and-dive movement is called porpoising.

To breathe while swimming dolphins leap out of the water as they are moving. This way they do not have to slow down to breathe.

Most humans find it hard to hold their breath for more than a minute. A dolphin can do it easily for 15 minutes!

Calves whistle to their mothers and other dolphins to let them know where they are, how they are feeling, or if they are frightened.

Voice box in throat

## IN THE KNOW

Every dolphin's whistle is unique, a bit like our voice. Underwater, dolphins use an air sac beneath their blowhole to make sounds. When they are in the air, they squeak by pushing air through the voice box in their throat.

# Wave Riders

Dolphins are built for swimming. They wave their tail up and down to move through the water and jump into the air. They twist their flippers to steer.

Dolphins will sometimes swim alongside ships and big whales. They ride the waves the ships and whales push out as they move.

## WOW!

A bottlenose dolphin can swim at 18.6 mph (30 kph). A human swimmer moves at about 4.3 mph (7 kph)

The dolphin's coat of blubber works like a lifejacket, making it float better in the water. Dolphins ride waves to save energy. Riding waves is similar to surfing at the beach, which dolphins do as well.

Bow wave from cargo ship

# My Gang

Dolphins live in a **pod** of about 15 adults and their children. When many pods get together, they form a superpod. All the dolphins mix together to meet new friends.

Dolphins love to play. They chase each other, do somersaults, and even play catch with seaweed.

## IN THE KNOW

The games dolphins play teach them swimming skills and help them find mates. The games get rough when strong **males** fight over the **females**.

Sometimes the games dolphins play can be rough and dolphins can get hurt.

Most dolphins have many scratches on their skin.

# Sensing the World

Dolphins can see, hear, and smell like other mammals. However, life in water means these senses have to work in very different ways.

The ear is hidden inside the head.

A dolphin has no nose.

The eyes look in two directions at the same time.

Sounds are picked up by the lower jaw bone.

Dolphins can hear underwater. They can hear birds splashing on the surface, creatures scuttling on the seabed, and schools of fish swimming by.

A dolphin does not smell through its blowhole. Instead it picks up smells in the water with its tongue.

Dolphins have **taste buds** on their tongue, like humans.

# Feeling out Food

*Boto dolphins live in the murky waters of South America's big rivers. They can see well, but they also use the bristles on their beaks for feeling out food on the muddy riverbed.*

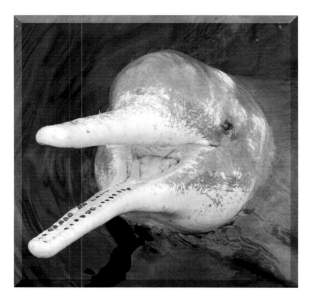

# Seeing With Sound

It is often dark and hard to see in deep water, so dolphins use sound to find out what is around them. They produce loud calls, which echo off the seabed and other animals in the area. This is called **echolocation**.

Dolphins use their whistles to help them navigate dark waters. The echoes they make can tell them a lot. Hard rocks and soft fish produce very different echoes.

Dolphins cannot see the color blue.

# How Echolocation works

*A dolphin makes loud ultrasounds. The sounds are too high for humans to hear. The sound echoes off a fish. The dolphin can then tell where the fish is and how large it is.*

The call is directed forward by the "melon," a bag of oily jelly inside the head.

Ultrasound call

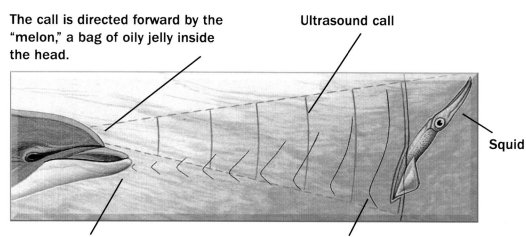

Squid

The dolphin picks up the echo with its jaw bone.

The ultrasound echos back from the squid.

## WOW!

Echolocation can even let dolphins see inside animals, including other dolphins!

# A Fishing Trip

Dolphins are hunters. They are ready to attack at any time of the day or night. Pods often work together to round up as much food as possible.

Dolphins use their senses to find food. They can hear large schools of fish swimming and they can use echolocation to find the schools.

A tight ball of fish is called a bait ball.

Dolphins work together to catch fish. They circle schools of fish. The fish try to swim away but end up trapped in the middle of the pod.

Some bottlenose dolphins hold a sponge in their mouth while they look for food on the seabed. The sponge stops them scratching their snouts.

Dolphins can chase fish up onto the shore. The fish flop in the sand and the dolphins leap up to the beach and eat them.

Dolphins can leap onto sandy banks to snap up the stranded fish.

# Snapping Up Food

Dolphins are not fussy eaters. They eat just about anything they can catch! Dolphins make it look easy, but it takes a lot of skill and practice to catch a meal under the sea.

Dolphins take turns swimming through the ball of fish. If the fish start to escape they will make a sound alerting the other dolphins.

Fast-swimming fish are stunned with a wave of sound to make them easier to catch.

## FAVORITE FOOD

**Shellfish**

**Lobster**

**Squid**

**Fish**

Dolphins grab fish in their mouths and kill them with one bite. Dolphins can eat a whole fish in one big gulp.

The dolphin's curved teeth hook into prey.

# Meeting Humans

When dolphins are close
to the coast, they may meet
humans. Some divers like
to swim with dolphins and
play with them, too.

Dolphins are friendly and
are not afraid of people.
They will let people pet
them, if they are gentle.

Dolphins are social animals. They live and play in groups and so they are happy to spend time with people, too. When one dolphin is hurt, the rest of the pod will help. Dolphins have been known to rescue drowning humans.

# Dolphins to the Rescue!

*Dolphins can learn tricks and be trained. The US **military** uses trained dolphins to find bombs in the water near ships and rescue swimmers who are lost or trapped.*

This dolphin has a camera on its flipper that records what the dolphin is looking at on the seabed.

# Taking a Rest

Dolphins have very large brains. They use it to make sense of all the sounds they hear in the water. Like all animals, dolphins needs to rest their brain by sleeping. However, they cannot sleep too deeply or they will stop swimming and drown!

Dolphins find quiet places to sleep. They do not go completely to sleep. They still have to swim to the surface to breathe.

Each half of a dolphin's brain takes turns sleeping for a few hours. As well as controlling swimming, the half brain is alert to **predators**, such as this bull shark. This big shark will try to bite a sleeping dolphin's tail off so it cannot swim away.

A bottlenose dolphin's brain weighs 3.7 lbs (1.7 kg). That is the same as 14 bananas and a little heavier than a human brain. A dolphin's body is also much bigger than a human's, but that does not mean they are smarter than us. Scientists think the bottlenose dolphin is the next smartest animal after people.

Dolphins fight off small sharks by headbutting their gill slits, but they stay as far away as possible from a powerful bull shark like this.

# Meeting a Mate

When a female dolphin is ready to breed, she mates with several of the males in the pod. If she meets a new pod she may choose to live and mate with some new companions.

Male dolphins will blow bubbles to attract a female's attention.

## IN THE KNOW

Female bottlenose dolphins are ready to breed once they are almost fully grown. It can take anywhere between seven and 12 years to reach the right size. A female dolphin could have as many as ten calves in her life.

When dolphins are ready to mate they play with each other and bump heads.

# WOW!

It takes 12 months for a dolphin calf to develop inside its mother. Human babies are born after about 9 months.

# Saving Dolphins

The bottlenose dolphin is one of the most common types of dolphin in the world. But many other types of dolphin are **endangered**. If people do not help them, some of them could become **extinct**.

Dolphins look for large schools of fish, and so do fishing boats. Sometimes dolphins get caught in fishing nets. They can't reach the surface to breathe and drown. Fishing with smaller nets and lines is safer for dolphins.

Many fishing boats use huge nets to catch fish. This dolphin was lucky not to get caught.

When dolphins or whales are stranded, they need to be helped back into the water or they will die.

Ship engines, jet skis, and even oil rigs make a lot of noise underwater. This can confuse dolphins. It could be one reason why dolphins sometimes get stranded on beaches.

太地よ、恥を知れ！
SHAME ON TAIJI

A few countries, such as Japan, still allow dolphin hunts. These people are protesting about it, saying that governments should ban the hunts.

# QUIZ

1) What does a dolphin use its lower jaw for?

2) Without a nose, what do dolphins use for smelling?

3) Dolphins ride bow waves of a ship a) to keep cool; b) save energy; c) listen to what people are saying?

4) How do dolphins stun fish?

5) What is a bait ball?

6) The name of a group of dolphins is a bop. True or false?

7) Why do dolphins die in fishing nets?

Answers:
1) A dolphin uses its lower jaw for hearing sounds.
2) Dolphins use their tongues for smelling.
3) b – to save energy.
4) Dolphins stun fish with a loud noise.
5) A bait ball is a shoal of fish trapped by dolphins.
6) False, it is a pod.
7) They cannot breathe and drown.

# GLOSSARY

**dorsal** (DOR-sul) To do with the back. A dolphin's dorsal fin is on its back.

**echolocation** (eh-koh-loh-KAY-shun) Bouncing sounds off objects to make echoes that tell an animal what is around it.

**endangered** (in-DAYN-jerd) When someting is in danger.

**extinct** (ik-STINGKT) When all of one type of animal, or species, dies out forever.

**females** (FEE-mayl) An animal that lays eggs or gives birth to young. The opposite type is a male, which cannot produce eggs or babies.

**fluke** (FLOOK) The fins on a dolphin's tail that point sideways.

**male** (MAYL) An animal that does not lay eggs or give birth to young, but must mate with a female before she can be a mother.

**mammals** (MA-mulz) An animal that feeds its babies milk and has at least a few hairs (dolphins have a few in their blowhole).

**military** (MIH-luh-ter-ree) Organizations that fight wars using soldiers, ships, or aircraft.

**pod** (POD) A group of dolphins or whales.

**predator** (PREH-duh-ter) An animal that hunts for other animals and then kills them for food. Dolphins are predators.

**prey** (PRAY) An animal that is hunted or killed by another for food.

**taste buds** (TAYST BUDZ) Sensors on the tongue that pick up the taste of food.

# Index

# Web Sites

Due to the changing nature of Internet links, PowerKids Press has developed an online list of Web sites related to the subject of this book. This site is updated regularly. Please use this link to access the list:

powerkidslinks.com/insti/dolphin/

D0126075